MW01714965

BE GRACIOUS TO ME

DAILY DEVOTIONS

JONATHAN W. SCHKADE

Copyright © 2023 Concordia Publishing House
3558 S. Jefferson Ave., St. Louis, MO 63118-3968
1-800-325-3040 • cph.org

Manufactured in the United States of America

1 2 3 4 5 6 7 8 9 10 32 31 30 29 28 27 26 25 24 23

Ash Wednesday and the Days Following

The Poor Ones

Read Psalm 41

> Blessed is the one who considers the poor! In the day of trouble the Lord delivers him; the Lord protects him and keeps him alive; he is called blessed in the land; You do not give him up to the will of his enemies. (Psalm 41:1–2)

Whenever the Bible proclaims, "Blessed is . . ." or "Blessed are . . . ," I assume it's talking about someone else. While I want to be "the one" blessed, do I really qualify? Do I consider the poor enough? Am I meek? Do I trust in the Lord the way I should? Not really. That's the problem with trying to earn blessedness. In reality, when we're blessed, it's only because God makes us who we need to be to be blessed.

All we are and possess on earth will turn to dust and ashes, making us "the poor" from Psalm 41:1. We need 2 Corinthians 8:9: "For you know the grace of our Lord Jesus Christ, that though He was rich, yet for your sake He became poor, so that you by His poverty might become rich." Because of this, we can now care for our neighbors' physical and spiritual poverty. More crucially, we can consider Christ, who became "the poor" so that our bodies will one day be raised from dust and ashes. He is the One God delivered from death, the One we call blessed, even as we receive His blessings.

We praise Your name, O Christ, blessed Son of the Father, through whom we are blessed! Amen.

Where Is Their God?

Read Joel 2:12–19

> Spare Your people, O Lord, and make not Your heritage a reproach, a byword among the nations. Why should they say among the peoples, "Where is their God?" (Joel 2:17)

Hello, God? Are You there? Do You even care? Both unbelievers and Christians ask such questions when awful things happen, and so little good seems to come from them. Proof that we live in a fallen, broken world is often treated as proof that God doesn't care. But that's backward. Horrible things happening should instead be proof of how hopeless we are without the one true God.

Human sin brought death, decay, and disaster into the world. God allows these bad things to happen, but He uses them for good and to remind us of our desperate need for Him. God shows us that we can help others who suffer. We can share the peace that Christ's death has won our resurrection. We can be inspired by the faith of those who persevere through hurt and face the idea that earthly death is not a permanent end. Seeing the effects of sin and death should lead us to repentance for our lack of trust. It should lead us to rely on Him with our hearts and actions. And when doubt and despair bow our heads, God wants to remove that burden so we can look up and see our God, who's been caring for us all along.

Father, forgive us when we doubt Your goodness. Have mercy on us sinners. In Jesus' name. Amen.

Becoming Sin

Read 2 Corinthians 5:20–6:10

> For our sake He made Him to be sin who knew no sin, so that in Him we might become the righteousness of God. (2 Corinthians 5:21)

What do you want to be when you grow up? Here's one good answer: forgiven. We should want this when we're young, old, and at all times in-between. No matter what incredible things we do with our lives, we still sin and do wrong against God and others. And sin isn't just something we do; being sinners was our core identity from birth. Sin consumed us. That's why, whatever else happens, we need to be forgiven, for that is how we will grow.

Fortunately, God could not let sin's conquest of us stand. His love for us compelled Him to take action. His love for us compelled Him to send His Son.

What do you want to be when you grow up? Jesus' answer: sin. And He achieved that goal by never sinning. He took all of our sin into Himself so that when He died on the cross, our sin, too, would be killed. And He turned us into something too: the righteousness of God: the opposite of what we were. Now we go forth as living contradictions of expectation—dying yet living, poor yet rich, "as having nothing, yet possessing everything" (2 Corinthians 6:10)—so others might see how God has changed us and be changed themselves.

Lord Jesus, thank You for becoming sin so we could be holy children of God. Amen.

Making a Show of It

Read Matthew 6:1–6, 16–21

> Beware of practicing your righteousness before other people in order to be seen by them, for then you will have no reward from your Father who is in heaven. (Matthew 6:1)

Have you ever seen a truly captivating performance? Perhaps it was a singer whose voice climbs to impossibly high notes or a magician pulling off a seemingly impossible illusion. Great entertainers know how to keep every eye on them and rake in the glory.

In His ministry, Jesus demonstrated the tools of a great showman. He spoke with authority. He drew large crowds and connected emotionally with them. And the wonders He did were beyond breathtaking. Jesus couldn't help but draw attention and praise. Still, He never did miracles or preached sermons for that reason. Sometimes He even told people not to talk about His amazing feats. Jesus didn't help people for personal glory but for His Father's glory. When Jesus gave to the poor and prayed and fasted, He honored His Father, who, in turn, honored Him.

We are to follow Jesus' example in giving, praying, and fasting. While we should never hide our acts of faith, we're not competing for the title of best Christian. "Righteous" acts done to bring ourselves praise aren't righteous or God-pleasing at all. Rather, we are to serve our neighbor and honor God, who deserves all praise and has already honored us by calling us His children.

Lord, lead us to honor You humbly with our words and actions. In Jesus' name. Amen.

Lent
Week One

Blessed Are the Poor

Luke 6:19–23

Blessed are you who are poor, for yours is the kingdom of God. (Luke 6:20)

The kingdom of God: that's a blessing anyone should be thrilled to receive! And all we have to do is be poor? That's not normally how our world works. The old saying is "The rich get richer and the poor get poorer." Being poor and being blessed seem like contradictions, yet Jesus puts them together.

We are, of course, poor in multiple senses. Though many of us are wealthy by earthly standards, our wealth is not anything we can keep beyond the grave. By God's measure of treasure, the eternal is what matters. Matthew's account of this sermon says "poor in spirit," meaning this blessing is for the spiritually humble, those who acknowledge their dreadful spiritual state and repent of it.

Consider Psalm 32:1: "Blessed is the one whose transgression is forgiven, whose sin is covered." There's no room in that for us to do anything but sin, to be spiritually poor. The rest is done to us and for us. It was done by Christ on the cross. It was done by the Spirit, working faith in our hearts. Because of that, to us belongs the kingdom of God. Of course, this kingdom belongs first and foremost to the Father and to Christ, His Son. It is because Jesus embraced our poverty that we receive His kingdom.

Blessed are You, O Christ, who gives us a home in Your kingdom, which shall not end. Amen.

Seeing Christ

Read Matthew 25:31–40

> And the King will answer them, "Truly, I say to you, as you did it to one of the least of these My brothers, you did it to Me." (Matthew 25:40)

The parable of the sheep and the goats—the separation and revelation of true believers and unbelievers—there's enough there for a week's worth of messages. We're going to stick with one simple point: when and where do we see Christ? The when is all the time, every day. The where is right before our eyes. It's among the lowly and suffering. Remember, Christ came in humility, a baby in Bethlehem, not a monarch in Jerusalem. He called fishermen and tax collectors, not scribes and princes. He touched the outcast and wounded, not the entitled and self-righteous. He knew hunger and thirst. He was a stranger. He was arrested and stripped of His clothes. Of course, we see Him best in the lowly.

We can see Christ in those He puts before us who hunger and thirst and hurt and need. He gives them as gifts for us to serve and love and share God's love with. Sometimes they are us as we struggle and scrape and cry for help. Christ saw someone worth caring for in each of us. He suffered and died to heal our sin-sickness and fill our needs. And He sees the faith God has given us and rejoices when we live out our faith by serving others.

Lord, help us serve others as You serve us. In Jesus' name. Amen.

Nothing Out of Everything

Read Philippians 2:1–11

Christ Jesus, who, though He was in the form of God,
did not count equality with God a thing to be grasped,
but emptied Himself, by taking the form of a servant,
being born in the likeness of men. (Philippians 2:5–7)

All knowing, always present, all powerful, and immortal King of heaven: that's what God is. That's what Jesus is. But knowing that we humans, through sin, were condemned to pain, corruption, and death, the Father sent His Son to save us, to be born as one of us.

Yet for Jesus to become one of us, for Him to do His Father's will through His earthly life and death, He had to empty Himself to become nothing. While still fully God, He gave up the benefits of being God. He chose not to use His power; He left His throne, made Himself mortal—able to die—and confined Himself to one specific place in one fragile body.

Humility is a hard concept to grasp. It's not weakness, though some see it that way. And it's far more than a lack of arrogance; it's the bestowing of worthiness on others. It's seeing their needs as greater than your own. Christ, who had all that's good in the universe, made Himself as nothing so that He could give us everything. Now dwelling in this grace, we can humbly share this Good News with all the world.

Lord Jesus, forgive our arrogance and bless us with spirits of humility and love. Amen.

Sick of Sickness

Read Psalm 41

> The LORD sustains him on his sickbed; in his illness You restore him to full health. (Psalm 41:3)

Yes, for those paying attention, this is the same Psalm as last Wednesday. It's the focus of our Lenten series and will repeat each week. As always, God's Word keeps coming before us with new insights as we become prepared to hear them. Today's focus is on verse 3.

How many of us, after a day or two of sickness, become sick of being sick? For those who suffer long-term illness, the painful tedium can be so much worse. "Heal me now, Lord!" we want to cry. While sometimes He does, at other times, the silent answer is "trust Me and wait." How hard those words are to hear! Know, however, that God is just as sick of sickness as we are. This consequence of sin in the world was never His desire. Though often He gives healing for sickness, sometimes He merely sustains us, guiding us through it, not past it. And even when healing does not come, God will not abandon us.

Whatever our health, the greater truth is that Jesus defeated the sickness of sin on the cross, breaking its hold on our hearts. That sin will be eradicated on the Last Day, taking with it all pain, all suffering forever. Then, full health in body and soul will be restored.

Lord, comfort those whose bodies ache for healing and help us minister to them. In Jesus' name. Amen.

An Attitude of Compassion

Read Psalm 103:1–14

He does not deal with us according to our sins, nor repay us according to our iniquities. (Psalm 103:10)

How many movies deal with payback? Something horrible is done to one person, who slowly and—usually violently—gets revenge. Most people cheer the hero on as "justice" is served against those who did wrong. How fortunate we are that God isn't like those movie heroes! After all, our sins would cast us as villains.

For thousands of years, humankind has sinned against God. Worshiping false gods, murdering, casually defiling His name, defying His every command—we've earned massive payback. His Son even died because of us. If our all-powerful God truly repaid us for our transgressions against Him, we'd be toast.

But Psalm 103 shows a God whose every action is led by mercy for sinners, mercy for us. Instead of seeking revenge for what we've done against Him, God sees how our sins destroy us, how they condemn us to death and hell. He sees our sin and suffering and gives us wildly undeserved compassion. That's why His Son died on the cross. We didn't have the power to make Him die. Rather than getting payback on us, He paid back the price we owed for our sins. Parents have compassion on their children because they are their children. How blessed we are that the Father sees all who fear and love Him as His children.

Have mercy on us, Lord, and cleanse our sins, for Jesus' sake. Amen.

An Attitude of Patience

Read James 5:7–18

> As an example of suffering and patience, brothers, take the prophets who spoke in the name of the Lord. Behold, we consider those blessed who remained steadfast. (James 5:10–11)

"Just deal with it." "Get over it." Have words like those ever helped anyone feel better? It's like hearing, "Hey, I know there's this huge problem in your life, but can't you just pretend it's not there anymore, that it doesn't hurt anymore?" Many problems simply won't go away overnight. Despite our best efforts and most fervent prayers, the pain continues.

God's compassion has no limit, yet He calls us to be patient in our suffering. He doesn't just swoop in the moment trouble starts and tell us how it's going to end or end it on the spot. Instead, He advises how to deal with pain, with suffering. Patience, steadfastness, prayer, and song: these are the attitudes and actions the Scriptures recommend. It's not easy to live out such advice, but that's where we ask the Holy Spirit to strengthen our faith.

An attitude of patience—and even one of joy—may not remove our suffering. It will, however, help us bear up under it, and it shows others a powerful witness of the One who will end our need for patience. He is the One who patiently waits for our repentance and who patiently forgives us each time we fail to be patient with others.

Lord, strengthen those who suffer as they await Your healing. In Jesus' name. Amen.

A Need to Be Healed

Read Matthew 8:14–17

> How long, O Lord? Will You forget me forever? How long will You hide Your face from me? How long must I take counsel in my soul and have sorrow in my heart all the day? (Psalm 13:1–2)

Have you ever prayed these words from Psalm 13? They're so intimate, so heart-wrenching, so real. As our problems go on and on, we cry out, "How long?" It can be soul-crushing to have a need you're unsure will ever be met. But a serious disease or accident can create such needs in the blink of an eye.

Seeing someone whose compassion never ran dry must have been a delight. It was part of why people flocked to Jesus. More astounding still was that He could do what no one else could: heal the incurable and fix the unfixable ailments of the body. But this wasn't even the most important gift He gave. Christ offered spiritual healing—forgiveness—and the promise of bodies that won't ever be corrupted again. In healing, He fulfilled prophecy (God's promises), and He'll never stop doing so. Christ will continue to keep God's promises of earthly and eternal healing.

Truly, He died and rose to conquer the consequences of our sin: sickness, injury, suffering, and death. Christ will destroy all of these enemies of humanity on the Last Day. And our cry of "How long?" will rise no longer.

Lord, as You remember me, help me remember what You have done for me. In Jesus' name. Amen.

Lent
Week Two

Nailed It

Read Colossians 2:6–15

> And you, who were dead in your trespasses and the uncircumcision of your flesh, God made alive together with Him, having forgiven us all our trespasses, by canceling the record of debt that stood against us with its legal demands. This He set aside, nailing it to the cross. (Colossians 2:13–14)

A perfect 10. A clean sweep. A flawless victory. People aspire to but seldom achieve these goals. To do exactly what you set out to do in exactly the way you want to do it is simply perfection. And that is how Jesus Christ accomplished His mission to earn our salvation: perfectly.

He recruited the disciples He wanted, was baptized into the sins of the sinners He came to save—all of us—preached the message He wanted to preach, lived the sinless life He needed to live, and rode into the city where He chose to die. He embraced His Father's will to suffer, be crucified, and proclaim His victory in hell. Then He followed that up with a perfect ending: rising from the dead, showing His glory, and ascending into heaven. Flawless victory.

And that victory is now ours through Baptism into Christ, where we are marked, buried, and raised with Him. Those very sins that corrupted and condemned us were stripped from us and taken by Christ, who nailed them to the cross. He nailed it, and we receive the reward.

Jesus, cover us in Your perfection as we approach Your Father. Amen.

On His Deathbed

Read Luke 23:32–43

> There they crucified Him, and the criminals, one on His right and one on His left. And Jesus said, "Father, forgive them, for they know not what they do." (Luke 23:33–34)

Whether it's a formal debate, a casual argument, or a bunch of friends joking around, most people covet getting the last word. We want that final zinger that shuts the other person up, gets the big laugh, or wins the discussion. And there are few words people remember more than our actual last few words, the words spoken on our deathbed.

What will yours be? Will they be words of love, advice for those you leave behind, or perhaps a secret or a true deathbed confession of sins? When the day comes, we can all pray that our final conversations will be filled with faith for our loved ones to hear.

The cross was Jesus' deathbed, and He knew there were important things He needed to say. His mother needed to hear that He was looking out for her. The penitent thief needed to hear that paradise awaited him. All the witnesses needed to hear who He trusted with His soul. Unlike human deathbed confessions of sin, Jesus' confession was of forgiveness for others, for the very people crucifying Him, for us. He carried all of our burdens and frailties to the cross so that we might be sustained through faith and restored to new life.

Father, fill our mouths with confessions of faith and trust in You. In Jesus' name. Amen.

When We Die

Read Romans 8:31–39

> Neither death nor life, nor angels nor rulers, nor things present nor things to come, nor powers, nor height nor depth, nor anything else in all creation, will be able to separate us from the love of God in Christ Jesus our Lord. (Romans 8:38–39)

Is there anything harder than facing death, confronting the reality that someone we love is no longer here or that our own end is fast approaching? It's what our faith is supposed to be all about: knowing that death is not the end, that God will preserve us through even that, and that He has prepared something better for us than this life. But when our faces are pushed right up against the window to see it firsthand, it's a moment of true revelation. Do we believe what we say we believe?

Fear doesn't make faith invalid. Moments of worry don't erase years of trusting that God will provide. Our faith may be weak, but God's love isn't. And He does not want to let us go. Inseparable—us and God's love. That's what Jesus made us. That's where our faith resides, and those are words we can cling to: nothing, not even death itself, can separate us from God's love. The love of the all-powerful God of the universe surrounds us. Sin, the devil, and even death itself are powerless to take us from His arms.

Father, thank You for sending Your Son to unite us with love that surpasses sin and death. In His name we pray. Amen.

A Gracious God

Read Psalm 41

As for me, I said, "O Lord, be gracious to me; heal me, for I have sinned against You!" (Psalm 41:4)

"Why are you being so nice to me?" That's such a human question. Paranoia and skepticism certainly never make the list of divine qualities of God. Humans, though, are suspicious by nature. It's no wonder. Living in a world of sin and lies, we ourselves seldom do things without an ulterior motive. It's no wonder we ask why God would be gracious to those who've sinned against Him.

In Psalm 41, the "me" was originally King David, speaking of His own calamity and hope. We can easily hear ourselves speaking these words too. We know we need help, even when we doubt whether God will grant it. But these aren't just our words and David's. They also belong to the One all the Scriptures speak of: Christ. They're also His words.

How can this be when they say, "I have sinned against You"? They can because that's what it means to say that Christ has taken our place. He has taken our sins. He has taken our spot as accused, convicted, executed sinner, who faced death, the injury that cannot be healed. Yet His Father healed Him, raising Him back to life in a glorified body. God was gracious to Him. That's why God will surely be gracious to us as well: for Jesus' sake.

Father, help me to receive the forgiveness You graciously give through Jesus. Amen.

The Heavy Load

Read 2 Samuel 12:7–23

> Come to Me, all who labor and are heavy laden, and I will give you rest. Take My yoke upon you, and learn from Me, for I am gentle and lowly in heart, and you will find rest for your souls. (Matthew 11:28–29)

That reading from 2 Samuel is hard to handle. King David is supposed to be one of the great heroes of the faith, a standard to aspire to. But here, David had failed as a man, as a king, as one who'd chased after God's own heart. He'd failed about as miserably as any man can, and now his sin was before him, undeniable and bearing a terrible cost. The consequences were unthinkable—unfair, our human hearts would say—but they were the natural consequences of his actions. And accepting that heavy load, he confessed and was forgiven, though his sin still had earthly repercussions.

No matter how much better than David we think we are—and remember, David was praised for his pursuit of God's will—we sin atrociously. Whether we see them or not, our sins create a heavy load of consequences we, too, must bear. But before us is One who wants to take our burdens, to take the worst of our consequences, and replace them with blessings. He bears our sins and gives us comfort in His salvation. He will bring rest to our souls.

Thank You, Jesus, for carrying our load and giving us rest in You. Amen.

Called to Suffering

Read 1 Peter 2:19–25

> If when you do good and suffer for it you endure, this is a gracious thing in the sight of God. For to this you have been called, because Christ also suffered for you, leaving you an example, so that you might follow in His steps. (1 Peter 2:20–21)

Someone should have told Charlie Brown years ago that suffering doesn't only and always have to be a terrible thing. It can actually be good grief.

We often preach the comfort, the release from suffering, the joy that faith in Christ brings. While these are true gifts, less sought after—but just as inherent in the Christian life in this fallen world—is suffering. We're called to endure suffering for the sake of our faith, to be treated unjustly for the good we say or do.

Since we complain and make excuses when we're punished for the things we've done wrong, taking a punishment we truly don't deserve feels absurd. In all honestly, we always deserve punishment, for sin is never far from us, but to suffer for the Gospel should be a joy. Christ was called to suffering too, but unlike us, He never deserved it. Still, He accepted the suffering, the mockery, the sins, and the death that rightly belonged to us. He embraced our suffering to make us righteous and able to stand before God as spotless lambs of our Good Shepherd.

Lord, uphold us to suffer graciously for Your Word. In Jesus' name. Amen.

Taking It Away

Read John 1:25–34

> The next day he [John the Baptist] saw Jesus coming toward him, and said, "Behold, the Lamb of God, who takes away the sin of the world!" (John 1:29)

We're usually not happy when people take things away from us. Our money, our time, our privileges, our loved ones—we don't want any of those taken from us. But when it comes to Christ taking away our sins, we're much happier. What do we really mean, though, when we say that Christ took all our sins away?

First, when Jesus takes something from us, He takes it forever. Through His perfect life and death on our behalf, Jesus took our stumbling and failing, our lies and blasphemies, our gossip and nasty remarks about people. He took our jealousy, our gluttony, our idle hands, and our most wicked thoughts. He even took away our burdens, our grief, and, especially, our sin. He said, "Those are mine to carry." And He didn't remove them and leave us empty. He refilled us with faith, love, hope, redemption, and joy. He filled us with His Holy Spirit, who creates a new spirit within us to live a life not defined by shame and evil. While we still sin, the punishment has been lifted from us. Standing before our Father's judgment, having our sins taken away, makes the difference between heaven and hell, between eternal life and eternal suffering.

Lord Jesus, thank You for taking away our sins and giving us Your Spirit. Amen.

Lent
Week Three

The Struggle

Read Romans 7:14–25

> For I know that nothing good dwells in me, that is, in my flesh. For I have the desire to do what is right, but not the ability to carry it out. For I do not do the good I want, but the evil I do not want is what I keep on doing. (Romans 7:18–19)

Here we are: forgiven, redeemed by Christ, living new lives as His children. And what do we do each day anew? We sin. We struggle. We fail. Our old nature and our new nature wrestle and shout against each other for dominance. And with startling strength, our old nature wins over and over again. No matter how much we struggle and squirm and deny it to ourselves, we sin.

Though it's not what we should be, it is our reality. From it, Christ calls us to repent, to receive mercy, to forgive and be forgiven, though we don't deserve it. He knows that we're helpless without Him and that our best efforts are futile—and it's important we know that too. The struggle continues every day of our earthly lives, but it will end. The fact that we struggle at all is a gift from God. Our sins show us that our need for Christ—like our struggle to live for Him—is real. And it's a need He's pleased to fill, saving us from ourselves and letting us rely on Him instead.

Lord, be my strength when I fail, and draw me daily to repentance. In Jesus' name. Amen.

Sacrificing for Our Sin

Read Hebrews 4:14–5:10

> For we do not have a high priest who is unable to sympathize with our weaknesses, but one who in every respect has been tempted as we are, yet without sin. (Hebrews 4:15)

Think of the people who've sacrificed for you—perhaps parents, friends, or a spouse. Many of us pat ourselves on the back or say, "Woe is me," for our small sacrifices. But for some, the sacrifices are huge, like the parent working three thankless jobs to put food on the table or pay for a child's education, sacrificing health and happiness to give another a chance at a better life.

Still, it's hard for us to fully grasp true sacrifice. First, it's a choice, an intentional decision to gladly give up something for someone else. Second, a true sacrifice holds nothing back. That's the kind of sacrifice our great High Priest, Jesus, made. He offered Himself on the altar of the cross so that we would not die forever. We're incapable of sacrificing for our own sin.

Paying for sin required another who could stand between us and God's righteous fury at sin. It required a sacrifice far purer than us. It required God's Son, the sinless man, Jesus. Our High Priest does not stand in judgment over us. He understands what we are, having been tempted as we are, yet without sin. His sacrifice means a better life now and forever for all who believe in Him.

Jesus, help us trust in Your sacrifice for our redemption. Amen.

Speaking Our Confession

Read 1 John 1:5–10

> If we say we have no sin, we deceive ourselves, and the truth is not in us. If we confess our sins, He is faithful and just to forgive us our sins and to cleanse us from all unrighteousness. (1 John 1:8–9)

It's as obvious as the envy in our eyes, laziness in our bodies, and nasty tone in our criticisms. We need confession. Without it, our terrible twistedness tears us apart with guilt and godlessness.

What twisted minds we have that what should be a joy of Christian life is seen as a burden so paralyzing that we avoid it. We confess together in church, saying we're sinners and begging for forgiveness, which we're surely granted! But do we take time to truly think about where we've sinned and confess it to God? Sin is not, after all, only something we generally do; it's something we specifically do. Confessing specific sins to God, to a pastor, or to those we've sinned against—these are powerful moments. Yet we hide from them. Why? Because we don't want to admit fault? Because we are frightened that forgiveness won't be granted? Because we think our vulnerability will leave us wounded?

Fear not! Confession clears the air, cleans the wound, and, most important, opens our ears to hear God say, "You're forgiven. For the sake of My Son on the cross, you're forgiven for what troubles you most." Use this gift, and receive freedom!

Have mercy on us, Lord, and forgive our sins. In Jesus' name. Amen.

The Devil's Glee

Read Psalm 41

My enemies say of me in malice, "When will he die, and his name perish?" (Psalm 41:5)

Can you hear the glee in verse 5? Like a pack of hyenas, the enemies are dancing around, delighted to see their foe's demise. Our enemy, the devil, is certainly eager to bring about our spiritual death. Tempting us with physical lures that often destroy our bodies, and emotional and spiritual traps designed to lead us away from God, the devil would love nothing more than to see us suffering an eternal death in hell along with him. Even before that, the good reputations we seek to build would disintegrate around us as we slide into corruption for all the world to witness.

Can you imagine the devil's glee when these words from Psalm 41 applied to Jesus as He hung on the cross? The devil waited for Jesus' life and legacy to die together. Instead, the devil was defeated, and death was overturned with the resurrection. What's more, all who believe in Christ Jesus for salvation from sin were preserved through earthly death, saved from eternal death, and given a new reputation: Christ's own. His name was offered to us through His death and presented to us in Baptism. Christians—that's what we are. We're given Christ's identity as the Father's children, His purity as God's lambs, and His life in the kingdom that will never perish.

Christ, in Your life is our life, and in Your name our salvation! Amen.

Conspirators

Read Ephesians 6:10–20

> For we do not wrestle against flesh and blood, but against the rulers, against the authorities, against the cosmic powers over this present darkness, against the spiritual forces of evil in the heavenly places. (Ephesians 6:12)

Conspiracies are fun to read about, but they can be horrible to live through. In the end, Julius Caesar certainly wasn't a big conspiracy fan. While for most of us, a true life-threatening conspiracy isn't something we have to worry about, smaller versions abound. Have you ever felt conspired against? Even something as simple as two co-workers complaining about you or a sibling trying to get you in trouble can hurt. While we may have people who don't like us very much or even work against us, they're not our true enemies.

Our true enemies conspire against us constantly, working to destroy us from the inside out: sin, death, and the devil. These same enemies assaulted Christ, and He withstood their blows, finally smiting them with His perfect life, death, and resurrection. Stripped of their power, they still plot and scheme against us, but we have only to look to our Savior for help. He can, has, and will defeat them for us. Their conspiracy has failed, and dressed in faith, wielding God's Word, we stand triumphant over them with our Savior, the One they could never hope to overcome.

Lord Jesus, preserve us from the schemes of our enemies and of our own sinful hearts. In Your name and for Your sake. Amen.

A History of Triumph

Read Deuteronomy 7:17–26

> If you say in your heart, "These nations are greater than I. How can I dispossess them?" you shall not be afraid of them but you shall remember what the Lord your God did to Pharaoh and to all Egypt. (Deuteronomy 7:17–18)

The Israelites had seen it all: the mighty plagues, the cloud and fire leading them, the Red Sea parted, water from a rock, manna on the ground each day, healing from serpents, and mighty armies defeated by God's power. Still, God knew that they doubted. It was what they'd done time and again. Here, He wanted to destroy all doubt that, as they took possession of the Promised Land, He would drive out their enemies.

Miracles abound in our lives as well; the fact that we're alive at all is one. So why do we doubt so often that the Lord will do as He said? That He has already done what He said? It's because we're sinners. We know we're not trustworthy, so it's easy to imagine that God isn't either. Yet the Lord has shown He will triumph over our adversaries—maybe not in the moment and way we want, but He will win. We know this because Christ has already won the victory on the cross over sin, death, and Satan. No matter what opposes us, He promises to love us and keep us safe forever. His Word is most certainly true.

Father, use Your Word in us to lead us in Your way. In Jesus' name. Amen.

A Vision of Victory

Read Revelation 19:11–16

> Now the salvation and the power and the kingdom of our God and the authority of His Christ have come, for the accuser of our brothers has been thrown down, who accuses them day and night before our God. (Revelation 12:10)

What does defeat look like? Perhaps it's an athlete blankly staring while opponents celebrate or a worker cursing silently while a rival is promoted. Or picture Adam and Eve expelled from the Garden of Eden, Goliath dead on the ground while the Philistines panic, or the Israelites trudging into exile, thinking they might never return.

For us, it's a little defeat each time we succumb to temptation, listening to that inner voice pleading, "It's not so bad. Do it just one more time." Blessedly, we know that God forgives those defeats and urges us to keep going, to try again, and to repent again. The devil thought mankind's defeat looked like Jesus hanging on the cross. But oh, how wrong he was.

That was actually a victory for us, and Christ literally went to hell to proclaim it before rising to life to proclaim it on earth as well. Revelation 19 gives another view of Christ's ultimate victory, showing the Word of God triumphant, terrifying to His enemies and beyond beautiful to His followers. It's with this vision of victory that we go forth, proclaiming His triumph and calling sinners to join us, marching under His banner of love.

Praise to You, Lord Jesus, for Your victory over all evil. Amen.

Lent
Week Four

Christ Remains Forever

Read John 12:23–36

> **So the crowd answered Him, "We have heard from the Law that the Christ remains forever. How can you say that the Son of Man must be lifted up? Who is this Son of Man?" (John 12:34)**

As Holy Week passed and Jesus neared the cross, He knew what was coming. No opponent tricked Him. No delusion filled His mind. No other vision guided His steps. He came to earth for the cross. He was born for the cross, prepared His disciples for His death, and entered Jerusalem to die. He chose the cross. Why would He turn aside now?

But when He spoke of His death, the people asked an interesting question: how could He die—"be lifted up" on the cross—and still remain forever, as was prophesied? Jesus didn't answer directly. Rather, He told them to focus on the present, on the blessing He was to them at that very moment. They were to walk in that light, to take it in, and to be children of light.

We also ask how we can die and still remain forever. And the answer is the same for us. Christ's resurrection, which we are tied into through Baptism, will come for us too. Just as He went to heaven, not staying among His disciples, so shall we live in heaven, remaining forever in a home far better than what this present earth provides.

Lord Jesus, thank You for choosing death so You could give us life. Amen.

From Cradle to Grave

Read Psalm 139:1–16

> Your eyes saw my unformed substance; in Your book were written, every one of them, the days that were formed for me, when as yet there was none of them. (Psalm 139:16)

God knows us every step of the way. He knew who we would be before our grandparents even met. He formed us in the womb and knew how we would turn out. He knew before our first breath exactly when our last breath would come. God knows it all.

He gives us these lives to live with choices we can make each day that affect our own lives and others, and He uses those choices to try to lead us to the best outcome. We can choose death. We can choose to end the gift of life God gives us, but we can't force our lives to extend one moment beyond what God wishes to give.

And the life He most wants to give us is the renewed spiritual life of faith in His Son. This is a life of abundance, not focused on worry for what each day may bring. God sent His Son so that death will not be permanent for those who believe in Him for salvation. For God knows when we'll die, and His hand is upon His children so that when that moment comes, He'll be ready to take us in His arms and carry us into His eternal home.

Father, what a joy it is to be known and loved by You! In Jesus' name. Amen.

Never Forgotten

Read Isaiah 49:13–16

> Can a woman forget her nursing child, that she should have no compassion on the son of her womb? Even these may forget, yet I will not forget you. (Isaiah 49:15)

Most of us have a story of being forgotten: our parents pulling out of the driveway without us, friends forgetting our birthday, or someone who promised to help us not showing up. It feels awful to be forgotten, like we're not important enough to remember, like we're not loved as much as we thought.

Old Testament Israel sometimes wondered if God had forgotten them. Believers throughout the centuries have wondered that too. It makes sense when thought of in human terms. Our memories are poor, and our willingness and ability to act on what we remember are ever poorer. But God does not forget us. He's incapable of doing so. And when He wants to act on what He remembers, He does so easily and decisively. He's almighty, after all.

God will never let our name, our memory, or, indeed, our very lives be forgotten. Rather, He keeps us alive literally and in His mind at all times. God is capable of that! For Jesus' sake, He remembers us. And remembering us, He acts on our behalf. He chooses to forget our sins, which have been wiped clean by Christ, and to remember always and only His deep love for us.

Remember me, Father, and help me remember all You have done for me through Jesus. Amen.

Betrayed

Read Psalm 41

> And when one comes to see me, he utters empty words, while his heart gathers iniquity; when he goes out, he tells it abroad. (Psalm 41:6)

The verse above is like a man visiting a colleague in the hospital. In the room, he says, "Hey, buddy, we're all rooting for you. And you look amazing, by the way." Then he goes back to work and says, "He looks terrible. And if he doesn't pull through, yours truly is in line for his office." Empty words equal faint comfort.

Have you ever been betrayed? Hurts, doesn't it? Jesus knows all about betrayal. His friend and follower betrayed Him for a few pieces of silver. With a kiss, a sign of friendship, Judas identified Jesus to the crowd who had come to arrest Him that night. Of course, Judas wasn't the only one to betray Jesus. Peter denied Him three times. The other disciples fled into the night.

And we betray Him every single day by sinning, thumbing our noses at the new lives of faith He suffered and died to earn for us. It's like saying, "Thanks for nothing, Jesus." How astounding it is, then, that God faithfully and consistently forgives our betrayals and responds to them with love. He points to His Son on the cross, who died so that our betrayals could be undone and our guilt erased forever. No matter what happens, He will never betray us.

Lord, forgive me when I sin against You, and remove my iniquity. In Jesus' name. Amen.

A Sharp Tongue

Read Psalm 52

> Your tongue plots destruction, like a sharp razor, you worker of deceit. You love evil more than good, and lying more than speaking what is right. (Psalm 52:2–3)

A tongue, like a razor, "lying more than speaking what is right." Who does that sound like? A politician, a con artist, or a shady lawyer? We've all known people with a sharp tongue and a willingness to say whatever it takes to destroy their opponent. Most of us have suffered injuries from such a weapon and possibly rebuffed them with nasty words of our own. Words can certainly destroy. They demolish morale, friendships, and reputations far faster than those can be built.

This psalm perfectly describes many of the Pharisees and religious leaders during Jesus' ministry. During His trial, a wild number of schemes and lies were thrown about in desperation to condemn Jesus for crimes He didn't commit. Jesus' reaction was the opposite: No scheming, just loving intentions. No evil, just good. No destructive words, just truth. Repeatedly during His ministry, Jesus silenced tongues that spoke against Him with profound truth. And His Word, with which He silenced Satan, is our tool for silencing the devil and our sinful nature. Instead, we listen to Christ, knowing that someday we'll hear "every tongue confess that Jesus Christ is Lord" (Philippians 2:11). And blessed are we, for our voices need not wait to proclaim that glorious truth.

Lord, guard our tongues from evil and fill our mouths with Your praise. In Jesus' name. Amen.

Teaching the Word

Read James 3:1–10

> Not many of you should become teachers, my brothers, for you know that we who teach will be judged with greater strictness. (James 3:1)

Teaching God's Word is a high calling. Pastors train for a long time to do this. Christian teachers, DCEs, and others do too. Even Sunday School and Bible study teachers study carefully before they teach. For every ten thousand perfect words, all it takes is a handful to undo the good that was shared. That's pressure! Parents aren't off the hook either, for it's primarily their job to teach their children about the Christian faith.

So how are all who teach, especially those who teach publicly, expected to fight back the impulses of pride, anger, and sloppy words to make sure they speak God's truth rightly? They do it through prayer, study, and trusting in the Spirit for guidance. And, of course, all who teach know they will fail at times. They are human beings, after all. Their words and attitudes are not perfect. But acknowledging this and asking for forgiveness when wrong can preach a powerful message too. Only one man ever spoke God's truth perfectly and obediently every time. And we know His name. It is the name above every name—the one we preach and teach and confess. It is His Word that we speak and His grace and mercy that empowers our teaching and forgives our mistakes. It is Jesus.

Father, bless those who teach Your Word with wisdom and courage. In Jesus' name. Amen.

Timid

Read Matthew 26:57–75

> Another servant girl saw him [Peter], and she said to the bystanders, "This man was with Jesus of Nazareth." And again he denied it with an oath: "I do not know the man." (Matthew 26:71–72)

"Timid." That's a word rarely used to describe Simon Peter. "Bold." "Brash." "Boisterous," even. Comparatively, "timid" hardly seems apt. But here, when it counted, when a proclamation of faith claiming Jesus as His Teacher and Lord could have amazed people, Peter swore lies instead. Big, brave Peter became timid. Fear does that to people. How bravely we speak God's promises to other Christians! But put us in a crowd of hostile unbelievers—like the one Peter faced—and many of us clam up about our faith. It somehow doesn't feel like the right moment to declare Christ as Lord.

Jesus was humble and sometimes silent, but He was never timid. Every word and action spoke boldly of His power, of His Father's plan of salvation, and of His concern for us. A timid man doesn't ride into a city to face an agonizing death at His enemies' hands. A timid man doesn't embrace thorns and whips and nails and asphyxiation on the cross when He could simply walk away. God wasn't timid in sending His Son, and Jesus wasn't timid in dying for our sins. Through faith, claim His boldness and announce to the world what He has done. It's a message they need to hear.

Embolden us, Lord, to speak Your Word when it matters most. In Jesus' name. Amen.

Lent
Week Five

The Church

Read Ephesians 4:1–16

> There is one body and one Spirit—just as you were called to the one hope that belongs to your call. (Ephesians 4:4)

Having a home to go back to can mean everything. Just ask someone who's been deployed away from family overseas or in the hospital for an extended period. We all want a place to belong. Of course, some people do not feel safe at home. Instead, relationships have frayed, and hurt has been inflicted. For both sets of people, there's another home right here on earth.

When God's Word works faith in the hearts of believers, God doesn't leave them in isolation. Instead, the Holy Spirit calls us to one Body, the Church, a home prepared by Christ Himself. For most of us, the first visible sign of this is a specific congregation, with a building and services and classes and believers we can talk to and bond with. This is good. Faith grows best when it's shared in community.

We may be in our lowercase-*c* church for life or we may move from one to another. But we remain part of the uppercase-*C* Church, the whole community of believers on earth and in heaven, for all time and in all places. In the Church, we receive His gifts, grow in faith, and speak in love, knowing that God's Word is sure and certain. There's always a place for us there.

Father, thank You for giving me a home in the Body of Christ, the Church. In Jesus' name. Amen.

Witnesses to the Truth

Read John 5:30–47

> You search the Scriptures because you think that in them you have eternal life; and it is they that bear witness about Me. (John 5:39)

Search the Scriptures, and you'll find Christ. He's what the Bible is about: the revelation of the Messiah, God's Son, who would save the world from its sins. In Eden, God promised One who would crush the serpent's head. In Genesis 12:3, God told Abraham, "In you all the families of the earth shall be blessed." In 2 Samuel 7, God promised that David's descendant would build a kingdom that would last forever. Isaiah, Zechariah, Micah, and others prophesied about who Jesus was and what He would do.

So when John the Baptist spoke of the Lamb of God (see John 1:29, 36), he stood in a long line of witnesses speaking with one voice. These and all of God's Word speak of Jesus, for He is the living Word. Sometimes, He rises to the surface of the Scriptures with clear proclamation, and sometimes, He is hidden deeper in the text, but He is there, speaking and being spoken about. And when Jesus Himself was born as one of us and preached God's Word Himself, many still didn't listen to what He said: His truth. We speak it, too, on His behalf. Together with our fellow believers, both living and dead, we make up a great cloud of witnesses proclaiming the message that saved us all.

Father, continue showing me all that Your Son has done for me. In His name. Amen.

The Devil's Lies

Read Matthew 4:1–11

> The tempter came and said to Him, "If You are the Son of God, command these stones to become loaves of bread." But He answered, "It is written, 'Man shall not live by bread alone, but by every word that comes from the mouth of God.'" (Matthew 4:3–4)

That devil is an amazing liar, isn't he? He takes a handful of truth, gives it a barely noticeable twist, and repackages it as an appealing lie. During Jesus' temptation in the wilderness, the devil was not playing games. He used his best lines. Jesus may have been suffering from forty days of hunger, but the devil never stood a chance. God's Word slew his lies.

The devil targets us now, tweaking and misapplying the truth with words that sound awfully appealing: "You can be like God and make your own rules." "God said He'll forgive you. Why not test that?" "God can't love you. You don't deserve it." On our own, we fall for it every time. But there is no need for us to be on our own. Christ is with us. He triumphed over the devil's temptations and sealed the victory on the cross. He will defeat him even now. With God's Word of truth living in our hearts, the devil has no place in us. His words are empty. His accusations are false. And God's promises are full and powerful to save.

Preserve us, Lord, by keeping Your powerful Word in our hearts and minds. In Jesus' name. Amen.

The End of Him

Read Psalm 41

> All who hate me whisper together about me; they imagine the worst for me. They say, "A deadly thing is poured out on him; he will not rise again from where he lies." (Psalm 41:7–8)

It's scary out there. For those who are true to God's Word, the world is becoming increasingly hostile. We're seen as out of step with progress, biased against other beliefs, and small-minded tyrants regarding the rights of others. It's an uncomfortable position to be in. And the world is certain that, in time, the teachings of the Scriptures can be coerced to match the world or discarded completely as more people look for another way. They yearn for the Church's end. But this is not the first time the Church has faced opposition.

Those who shouted for Jesus' crucifixion thought it would end Him. They thought they'd eliminated a dangerous foe forever. Instead, their sinful actions helped put Him exactly where He wanted to be: on the cross, dying to save sinners, including those who longed for His demise. Christ ended the reign of sin, death, and Satan and made a new beginning for us. He rose from the dead, proving His enemies wrong. And He gave hope a face and a name and a place to live in His Church. Now He makes peace with us, who were once His enemies, and brings us into His family and His kingdom.

Lord, keep us true to Your Word as You surely are true to us. In Jesus' name. Amen.

Why Do We Suffer?

Read Jeremiah 9:12–16, 23–24

> Why is the land ruined and laid waste like a wilderness, so that no one passes through? And the LORD says: "Because they have forsaken My law that I set before them, and have not obeyed My voice or walked in accord with it." (Jeremiah 9:12–13)

Why is the world broken? Why do so many horrible things happen and so many people suffer? Sin. Sin chosen once for all people by Adam and Eve. Sin chosen each day by each of us in thoughts, words, and actions. Many bad things are not a consequence of a specific choice or behavior. But they're still the result of sin, which breaks down everything that is good in the natural world and in our own bodies.

We can't just blame others. We too often see God's Law as suggestions that we happily break. In doing so, we condemn ourselves to the Law's punishment: death. We deny our sin and choke on its consequences, but the evidence shows we're liars. Sin rampages through the world, corrupting it, corrupting us, and there is only one escape. Not riches, nor might, nor wisdom, but the steadfast love of the Lord. Because God loves us, Christ came to fix our brokenness and suffer the death the Law sentenced us to. His Gospel message of salvation for all who believe in Him gives hope that can sustain us through earthly hardships.

Father, comfort those we love with healing in this broken world for Jesus' sake. Amen.

Sin's Greatest Hits

Read 2 Timothy 3:1–9

> The saying is trustworthy and deserving of full acceptance, that Christ Jesus came into the world to save sinners, of whom I am the foremost. (1 Timothy 1:15)

It's a punch to the gut: "For people will be lovers of self, lovers of money, proud, arrogant, abusive, disobedient to their parents, ungrateful . . ." and it goes on in 2 Timothy 3. Perhaps there are a few traits listed that we think we've avoided, but it mostly reads like a greatest hits list of our worst sins, including the ones we commit regularly. How are we not quivering in guilt?

Many of these sins abound in our society, as they have abounded in societies of the past. It's horrible. And Paul is telling us to avoid people who do such things. But how do we avoid ourselves when we, too, are guilty? The community of faith helps guard and protect us from the worst applications of these vices, and it's where we can be strengthened and encouraged in our faith. In those around us fighting the same battles, struggling with the same sins, and seeking forgiveness from the same Lord, we find brothers and sisters we can rely on and love. And yes, even when we fail, we still condemn those sins and extend love to those who need to repent. We pray for them, knowing we all need the mercy and grace of Christ's cross.

Father, forgive our sins and help us lead others to repentance. In Jesus' name. Amen.

Hearing and Believing

Read Matthew 26:1–5

> You know that after two days the Passover is coming, and the Son of Man will be delivered up to be crucified. (Matthew 26:2)

As a parent, I never underestimate the ability of my children to completely misunderstand direct statements. They're often shocked to learn that commands like "Be quiet while Mom naps" and "Load the dishwasher before supper" actually mean what they say. Jesus' disciples must have driven Him crazy. They often didn't listen. Or they seemed to think, "He can't really mean that. Let's pretend He means something else." Until His arrest, they remained skeptical about His crucifixion. They, like us, were masters at denying uncomfortable and unexpected truths.

Ironically, the ones who would have agreed with Jesus' revelation of His impending death were the very conspirators working to cause it. They missed—even more than the disciples—the purpose of Jesus' ministry. He wasn't interested in political or social power. He didn't care about overthrowing the Pharisees or chief priests or elders. He was focused on a more important task: His crucifixion for the sins of the world. Perhaps if they'd listened more closely to Him instead of to their fears and egos, they'd have heard the truth. We're also less than amazing at hearing and believing everything Jesus and His Word says. At times like that, all we can say are the words of Mark 9:24: "I believe; help my unbelief!"

Lord, give me faith to believe and confess all You have said in Your Word. In Jesus' name. Amen.

Holy Week

Going after Him

Read John 12:12–19

> So the Pharisees said to one another, "You see that you are gaining nothing. Look, the world has gone after Him." (John 12:19)

This is what the disciples had been waiting for: a triumphal procession with a large crowd proclaiming Jesus' greatness. They probably couldn't help but bask in it, feeling they'd had a hand in its happening.

To us, it seems right that the crowd gathered largely because Jesus had shown Himself to be the master over death by resurrecting Lazarus. If only the disciples had clung to that belief and its implications, there'd have been far less fear in their hearts during the following week. And how grand indeed if the Pharisee's words had been true, if the world had truly "gone after Him." But, as the next days showed, only some believed in Him as true followers. The rest, after their excitement waned, soon let their faith get trampled by fear.

How like the disciples we are: praising Jesus, hoping to experience secondhand glory, and often missing the point. But we still want to do what the Pharisees feared: go after Jesus. We want to lead others to do the same. He led the way through death, through the open tomb, and into heaven. This is a path we long to follow. It's a path He wants us, with Spirit-given faith, to follow: going after Him all the way to His Father's throne.

Lead us in Your way, Lord Jesus, to our Father's kingdom. Amen.

Living the Law

Read Matthew 22:34–40

> You shall love the LORD your God with all your heart and with all your soul and with all your might. (Deuteronomy 6:5)

Forget politicians or celebrities or athletes after the big game. When it comes to question-and-answer sessions, Jesus is the master. Consider all the times the scribes, Pharisees, or Sadducees came to Jesus with trick questions. The smartest religious guys of the age laid out trap after trap for Jesus, only to find themselves caught in these traps instead.

This time, in our reading from Matthew, the encounter is fairly straightforward, and the answer seems simple to understand. "Which is the great commandment in the Law?" (Matthew 27:36). Love the Lord completely. Love your neighbor as yourself. Got it. Simple to say, but impossibly hard to do. This, of course, is part of the point: we can never keep the Law. The implied next conclusion should be that we need someone else to keep the Law in our place.

Jesus kept both of these commandments perfectly. The fact that He sacrificed Himself in love for His Father's will and in love for His neighbor—us!—is the answer to all our problems. We fail at loving how we should, but, through the Spirit, we still try—striving to do better. We ask for God's help to live in the love we've received and to love those who need the life we live in.

Father, thank You for loving us enough to sacrifice Your Son to save us. In His name. Amen.

Preparing for the End

Read Matthew 24:3–14

> But the one who endures to the end will be saved. And this gospel of the kingdom will be proclaimed throughout the whole world as a testimony to all nations, and then the end will come. (Matthew 24:13–14)

Pretend that you're planning for an apocalyptic disaster, the kind seen in movies, where everything's normal until the bomb falls, the virus strikes, or the meteor hits. How would you prepare if the only resources you could be certain of were the ones you could gather ahead of time yourself?

Christ prepared for the end of His earthly ministry in numerous ways. He put Himself in the right place at the right time to carry out His Father's plan, He taught what His disciples would need to know after He died, and He preached to the crowds and did miracles to show His Father's glory. His best preparation was doing what He'd done all along: trusting His Father's will. This carried Him into a devastatingly painful death, but it also carried Him through His task of redemption. God's plan for the end saw Christ bursting from the grave so that we would also be prepared for the end of our lives and the end of this world. We prepare for the end by trusting in Him and doing as His Word says. Most of all, like Jesus, we prepare by saying to our Father, "Thy will be done."

Father, Your will be done in our lives and in our world. In Jesus' name. Amen.

Be Gracious to Me

Read Psalm 41

> But You, O Lord, be gracious to me, and raise me up,
> that I may repay them! (Psalm 41:10)

"Be gracious." It means to be kind and generous. In the Scriptures, it also means to show divine grace, the undeserved goodness and blessings only God is capable of giving. David prayed that God would restore his strength so he could repay his enemies. For Jesus, it had a deeper meaning. It meant resurrection—something that truly only God could do.

The days approaching Jesus' death could not have been easy. He knew betrayal and death were coming, and in the Garden of Gethsemane, His burden was apparent. He sweated blood. In a time like that, how important would the hope of verse 10 be? Extremely important. God's graciousness, His ability to raise Jesus up from death after He was raised up on the cross, was integral to the plan having a purpose at all. It's why Jesus' going forward into death was a full solution for our doomed state. It's also why we can go forward. For without a resurrection, our hope would be hollow.

We know we'll have troubles, injuries, personal disasters, and someday death befall us. But we, like Jesus, have the knowledge that God will be gracious to us and will raise us up, both from earthly calamities and from the grave. Our sleep of death will be no more permanent than Christ's was.

Lord, in You I put my hope, for You alone can raise me up. Amen.

A Higher Way

Read Isaiah 55

> For My thoughts are not your thoughts, neither are your ways My ways, declares the Lord. For as the heavens are higher than the earth, so are My ways higher than your ways and My thoughts than your thoughts. (Isaiah 55:8–9)

Our stubborn human brains are obsessed with understanding every detail of God's mind. There's good in that. Trying to know and do God's will, seeing others how He sees them—disciples should do that, and doing so increases our joy. But thinking we're capable of understanding every detail of God's plans is nuts. Realistically, we're not equipped to even attempt to halfway understand the plans of the all-knowing King of the universe. Fortunately, that's not our job. Our job is to trust Him as He has revealed Himself: a loving God who sacrificed His Son to redeem His people from sin.

When Christ was crucified, God's ways seemed mysterious and contradictory, but they were consistently focused on the cross leading to our resurrection. We couldn't have imagined this path to salvation. The innocent shouldn't suffer for the guilty. The judge shouldn't be the one condemned. The immortal shouldn't die. But that was God's way. It was the way for His life to become our life. And as the tomb awaits its opening, we can rest, knowing that we'll be resurrected and that His way will take us higher than our way ever could.

Father, guide me in Your way to believe the truth You've revealed. In Jesus' name. Amen.

What's His Is Ours

Read Romans 6:1–11

> We were buried therefore with Him by baptism into death, in order that, just as Christ was raised from the dead by the glory of the Father, we too might walk in newness of life. (Romans 6:4)

Hallelujah! What a victory! Christ, the Lamb who was slain, has been raised! And are we the same old sinners, the same walking corpses we were before? By no means! His death and new life have changed us forever, so let's go out with joy.

Before Christ, we were dead and buried, born in a grave of original, inherited sin. Every day, we dug the hole deeper, throwing more sin on top of our bodies, burying ourselves further into the ground. There was no way out, no changing our fate. We were dead and destined for damnation.

Then came Christ! Faith in our Savior made all the difference. Baptism into His holy name made all the difference, tying us inextricably into His life, death, and resurrection. His holiness made us holy. His death killed our cold hearts that could choose only sin. His resurrection pulled us from that eternal grave and breathed into us the air of hope and freedom. So shall we choose to live in sin again? Shall we jump back into that bottomless grave? Or shall we wrap our arms around Christ, embrace our new life in His forgiveness, and shout, "He is risen, and we, too, shall rise!"

Hallelujah, Lord Jesus, for You have made us new in Your resurrection! Amen.